SHARKS

– BUILT FOR THE HUNT –

by Tammy Gagne

raintree
a Capstone company — publishers for children

Raintree is an imprint of Capstone Global Library Limited, a company incorporated in England and Wales having its registered office at 264 Banbury Road, Oxford, OX2 7DY – Registered company number: 6695582

www.raintree.co.uk
myorders@raintree.co.uk

Editorial Credits
Brenda Haugen, editor; Kazuko Collins and Juliette Peters, designers;
Tracy Cummins, media researcher; Katy LaVigne, production specialist

Printed and bound in China.

ISBN 978 1 474 70196 9 (hardback)
19 18 17 16 15
10 9 8 7 6 5 4 3 2 1

ISBN 978 1 474 70203 4 (paperback)
20 19 18 17 16
10 9 8 7 6 5 4 3 2 1

British Library Cataloguing in Publication Data
A full catalogue record for this book is available from the British Library.

Photo Credits
Corbis: Thomas Kokta/Masterfile, 5; Getty Images: Dr. Klaus M. Stiefel /Pacificklaus Photography, 18, Jens Kuhfs, 21; Minden Pictures: Norbert Wu, 15; National Geographic Creative: NICK CALOYIANIS, 19; Science Source: Georgette Douwma, 17; SeaPics.com: Randy Morse, 7; Shutterstock: Derek Heasley, Back Cover, Matt9122, 13, Cover, Nantawat Chotsuwan, 2, pashabo, Design Element, Shane Gross, 1; SuperStock: NHPA, 3; Thinkstock: Jupiterimages, 11, webguzs, 9.

CONTENTS

ON THE HUNT

The mighty shark has spotted a sea lion. The shark moves closer as it circles its **prey**. Before the sea lion even senses any danger, bam! The shark speeds up and rams the helpless animal. This powerful move often stuns the prey. Sometimes it even kills the prey.

Sharks are known for being at the top of the ocean food chain. Sharks eat many other animals, but few animals eat sharks. Most sharks eat smaller fish. But some sharks also eat seals, sea lions and even whales.

FACT
Thresher sharks swat their tails at small fish to stun them before eating them.

prey animal hunted by another animal for food

MANY SIZES

Sharks can be many sizes. Spined pygmy sharks are one of the smallest sharks. They are only about 20 centimetres (8 inches) long. These tiny **predators** rely on their sharp teeth for catching prey such as small squid and shrimp. The blue shark is much bigger. It is about 3.8 metres (12.5 feet) long. It uses its size to overpower seabirds, seals and turtles.

The great white shark is the biggest predatory fish. It can grow up to 6 metres (20 feet) long and can weigh 1,905 kilograms (4,200 pounds)!

FACT
The bull shark has the strongest bite of all sharks. It can bite a sea turtle in half: shell and all!

predator animal that hunts other animals for food

blue shark

LIFE IN THE FAST LANE

Great white sharks have strong jaws. Few animals can escape the jaws of this powerful predator. Great whites are one of the fastest sharks. When chasing prey, they can swim up to 56 kilometres (35 miles) per hour.

Most sharks hunt alone. But dogfish sharks hunt in a pack, like wolves. Sometimes hundreds of sharks work together, attacking prey from below or behind. The other animals have little chance against such a large group.

FACT

Sharks rarely attack people. In 2014, there were only three deadly shark attacks in the world.

great white shark

CUTTING TEETH

Most animals have one row of teeth. Sharks have between 5 and 15 rows of teeth in each jaw. The spiky teeth are used to grab prey. Long, curved teeth prevent slippery fish from escaping. Some teeth are **serrated**, like knives. A shark uses these teeth for cutting into its food.

FACT

Sharks are always growing new teeth. When old ones fall out, new ones grow in their place. As the shark gets bigger, so do its teeth.

serrated saw-toothed

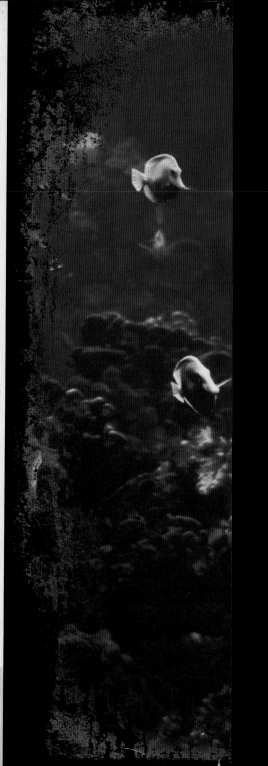

SEEK AND FIND

Sharks have **keen** senses. If prey is near, a shark will surely see or smell it. Sharks can see in the dark even better than cats can. This helps sharks to see in dark, murky water. But not even their eyesight can beat their sense of smell. When searching for food, they use this sense the most.

FACT

Sharks swing their heads from side to side when hunting. This movement helps them to follow the scent of their prey.

keen highly developed or extremely good

SPECIAL SENSES

Sharks have several dark dots on their faces, called **pores**. Scientists have found that these pores are part of a special sense. All living things give off electricity in the water. A shark's pores allow the predator to feel the electricity of its prey.

FACT

A shark can feel **vibrations** in the water. The vibrations let the shark know that another animal is approaching.

pore tiny hole in the skin

vibration fast movement back and forth

A FISH OUT OF WATER

A few types of shark are known for jumping out of the water. Mako sharks are among these skilled athletes. They can leap up to 9 metres (30 feet) out of the water. This ability helps them to chase prey such as seabirds or fish that jump out of the water.

FACT

A mako shark's body temperature is several degrees higher than the water around it. This **trait** gives the shark extra energy when chasing prey.

trait quality or characteristic that makes one animal different from another

AT HOME IN EVERY OCEAN

Many sharks prefer warm water, but some live in colder areas. Sharks live in every ocean. They can even be found in the Arctic and Antarctic regions. Some sharks **migrate** to warmer regions during the winter. They travel to where prey is most plentiful.

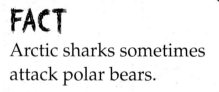

FACT

Arctic sharks sometimes attack polar bears.

migrate travel from one place to another; animals often migrate to find warmer weather

A Greenland shark swims
past an underwater ice ledge.

NIGHT HUNTERS

Most sharks are **nocturnal**. They hunt at night and during the early morning when prey fish are most active. Sharks also tend to move closer to land during these hours. If a shark finds a school of fish, it will often follow it towards the shore.

FACT

Sharks sleep by resting half of their brain at a time. This allows them to be alert at all times.

nocturnal active at night and resting during the day

AMAZING BUT TRUE!

Sharks can sense when a hurt animal is near by. Sharks can smell a single drop of blood in 25 million drops of ocean water. These fierce animals will even attack other wounded sharks.

GLOSSARY

keen highly developed or extremely good

migrate travel from one place to another; animals often migrate to find warmer weather

nocturnal active at night and resting during the day

pore tiny hole in the skin

predator animal that hunts other animals for food

prey animal hunted by another animal for food

serrated saw-toothed

trait quality or characteristic that makes one animal different from another

vibration fast movement back and forth

READ MORE

Shark vs Penguin (Predator vs Prey), Mary Meinking Chambers (Raintree, 2012)

Shocking Sharks (Walk on the Wild Side), Charlotte Guillain (Raintree, 2013)

Strange Sharks (Creatures of the Deep), Rachel Lynette (Raintree, 2012)

WEBSITES

www.bbc.co.uk/nature/life/Chondrichthyes

Learn more about sharks and other fish with similar skeletons.

www.bbc.co.uk/nature/life/Great_white_shark

Find out more about great white sharks.

www.ngkids.co.uk/did-you-know/great_white_sharks

Discover 10 fascinating facts about great white sharks.

COMPREHENSION QUESTIONS

1. Make a list of the abilities that make sharks powerful predators. Which ability do you think matters most?

2. How would the teeth shown on page 11 help a shark to catch prey?

INDEX